Stuttering

Help

A Guide to Simple Techniques Which You Can Use to Control Your Stutter so That You Can Speak Fluently and With Confidence

By Clark Darsey

Contents

Thank you for buying this book and I hope that you will find it useful. If you will want to share your thoughts on this book, you can do so by leaving a review on the Amazon page, it helps me out a lot.

Introduction

Stuttering is an embarrassing issue. When you are not able to communicate plainly, it affects every area of your life. It can hinder your relations with other individuals, and cause you to end up being withdrawn. You might be so ashamed by your speech that you speak as little as possible. You feel as if your speech is inadequate-- that you are not getting your point across.

If stuttering has actually been an issue for you, do not surrender hope-- there are options! You can discover how to take control of your speech, instead of enabling it to manage you!

There are lots of easy techniques to help manage your stuttering. When you browse through all of the possibilities, you ought to begin to feel confident. When you attempt these techniques, you will discover which ones work the best for you. From the convenience and personal privacy of your own home, you will find it really simple to master these techniques. You can then start to apply them to your daily speech to see how they work.

Even if you have actually stuttered for many years, these simple techniques will end up being useful solutions to your stuttering. They are going to help you to find out how to communicate plainly and successfully. Speaking with individuals, in groups, and even publicly, can be as satisfying as it was meant to be-- every single time without fail.

Mastering the simple techniques to manage your stutter can do marvels for your self-confidence. When you have found out the art of communicating properly, it will increase your self-confidence in your life.

Some individuals require a little extra assistance to manage their stuttering. Often there are unique circumstances that call for a special method in order to work. Whichever category describes you, they are all dealt with here within this book and you are bound to find something for you.

Read, learn, practice, and apply-- and clear, confident speech can be yours!

Chapter 1: You Can Utilize Easy Techniques to Manage Stuttering

For the majority of people who stutter, mastering some fundamental techniques is all they have to do. Stuttering does not need to ever be an issue again. All it takes is the dedication to try out these techniques, and discover which ones work the best for you. You might discover that you have to utilize a variety of methods in order to have effective speech. With a little practice, they are going to come naturally. You can anticipate a lifetime of confident speaking!

There are 2 essential points to bear in mind before you attempt these methods, and when you are practicing them. Initially, there is no one technique that works similarly well for everybody. This is why there are numerous techniques noted here. You have to try them all to discover which ones work ideally for you.

Second, whether your stuttering is extreme or minor, you can not acquire ideal, complete control over your stutter overnight. It requires practice and effort on your part, and it requires time for you to see the outcomes.

If you want to make this dedication and do not expect your stutter to vanish in a day, you will have the ability to find out which of these methods works for you. Your speech is going to no longer be a reason for shame or concern-- it can be among the most satisfying parts of your life!

Chapter 2: Think About What You Wish to Communicate

There is a lot more to speech than simply saying words. When you speak with somebody, you are trying to convey something. Possibly you are trying to get the point across, ask a question, or clarify something. Whenever you speak, there is a message in what you are saying. Considering what you want to communicate beforehand has advantages that can help you to manage your stuttering.

The message you want to offer has its own tone. It includes your state of mind, your mindset, your thoughts and feelings-- a lot more than simply words! What do you wish to say, and what do you hope the listener will get from it? It just takes a couple of minutes to think about these aspects before you start to speak.

Thinking of what you wish to communicate puts strength behind your message. It can additionally put strength behind your speech. The way this is done is it puts your focus on the significance of what you are saying-- why it is crucial. This focus can, in turn, divert your self-consciousness far from your speech. It might even get rid of it completely.

Instead of just saying words, which you might stumble on, you will be communicating your state of mind, mindset, and confidence, which accompanies it. You will be speaking plainly, instead of guarding your speech. With practice, this technique can help you to manage your stutter.

Chapter 3: Making and Sustaining Eye Contact

The individual who stutters typically establishes the routine of avoiding eye contact with individuals to whom he is speaking. He has actually ended up being so adapted to his faltering speech that he does not wish to see the response of the listener. This can cause you to end up being a lot more uneasy and stutter a lot more.

You can turn this unfavorable habit around to your favor. While it might take some practice, it is well worth the effort. When you are preparing to talk to somebody, make a point of making eye contact with him. You can start by reminding yourself that he truly does wish to hear whatever you intend to say. For the most part, you will get a spoken or unspoken affirmation of this, before you start to speak.

As you speak, hold eye contact with the individual. If you speak nicely and show this pleasant mindset in the eye contact instead of a vibrant gaze, you will see that he is listening enthusiastically to whatever you are saying to him.

This method can help you to establish the practice of valuing one-on-one interaction. It can aid you to concentrate on the interaction itself, instead of on your speech difficulty. You are going to gain control over your verbal communications, and discover them to be a lot more satisfying. As these habits begin to come naturally, your speech will additionally start to stream more naturally.

Chapter 4: Learning and Applying Deep Breathing to Your Speech

Appropriate breathing can play a considerable role in controlling your stutter. It is an excellent, healthy practice which you can start doing by yourself and put it into practical use.

You can start by mastering deep breathing on your own, in the privacy of your own house. Begin by taking slow, deep breaths, breathing in intentionally, and after that, breathing out just as slowly. Doing this in a calm, peaceful environment where you will not be disrupted by other individuals or outside noise is preferable. The fewer diversions you have, the better. Practice this simple, deep breathing method one or two times a day-- however long you require for it to feel natural like you have been doing it forever.

If you want, you can include a bit of rehearsal after you have actually found out how to do this. It can increase your confidence if you practice this brand-new technique on an inanimate object or your pet. While this might sound uncommon, you might be shocked at how well it can work! You can rehearse by incorporating this deep breathing method prior to, and throughout, your "conversation" with your pet. Do the deep breathing method before you start to speak and briefly throughout your "conversation."

Deep breathing throughout speech gives a variety of advantages. Initially, when your focus is taken off your speech and concentrated on your breathing, you will be more confident when you are speaking. In addition, deep breathing readies your body for a smooth, successful speech. It unwinds all of the muscles that you utilize when you are speaking, helping your speech to stream effortlessly.

After you have actually found out how to do this, you can try it out on another individual. It is necessary to remember that after you have mastered this practice, the individual you are talking to will most likely not even notice you are doing it. Your speech will be more deliberate, well-thought, and with less chance of stuttering.

Chapter 5: Establish an Excellent Sense of Humor

Stuttering is not funny. If you stutter, you already understand this. Nevertheless, even when you start finding out how to manage your stutter, you might periodically make blunders. The way you approach a mistake can make all the difference in the world-- not just to that one specific conversation but additionally in how you approach future conversations.

Having the ability to say "Oops!" and laugh at a blunder might not come effortlessly. This is particularly true if you have actually been mocked about your stuttering in the past. Nevertheless, a sense of humor about your stutter is the healthiest approach to establish.

Establishing a sense of humor about your stutter is something best started when you are alone while no one else is watching. Consider circumstances you have actually been in, when your stutter was especially irritating. Think about just how much better the ultimate result might have been if you had actually had the ability to laugh and make a joke out of it. It would not have appeared so terrible if it was handled properly.

Next, consider how you can integrate a sense of humor into future stuttering. Possibly you can think of it in the same terms as an unscripted bout of hiccups. If a hiccup would not lead you to end up being ashamed and flustered, neither should a stutter. Be ready for such situations because they will come inevitably.

Understanding that you are going to make mistakes is the very best way to be ready for them. In fact, acknowledging the possibility of a mistake makes it less probable for one to, in fact, happen. You recognize that you can not be perfect, and you are ready for what to do when you are not. You will not stress over stuttering, and verbal interaction will be a lot more pleasurable for yourself and for everybody else concerned.

Chapter 6: Calm Your Nerves

If you think of your history with stuttering, you might see just how much more of an issue it was whenever you were nervous. When you are nervous, you end up being awkward; when you are awkward, you are less in control. It can end up being a vicious cycle of uneasiness, inhibition, and loss of control over your stuttering.

Keeping yourself calm takes work and practice. If you are nervous by nature, or if your daily life frequently consists of scenarios that provoke uneasiness, it might take additional effort.

The calmer you have the ability to remain on a routine basis, the more control you will have over your stutter. As stuttering and stammering can be directly related to uneasiness, working on this issue can minimize your stuttering and provide you with more control. Teaching yourself to embrace a calm disposition and a positive outlook might not get rid of your stuttering, however, it can help to lower it.

In addition to these elements, particular products that you consume can additionally contribute to uneasiness. Caffeine is among the most frequent offenders. If you have the habit of consuming numerous servings of coffee, tea, or sodas throughout the day, switching to healthier, non-caffeinated drinks might be valuable. The restlessness which you feel after consuming a big amount of caffeine can impact every part of your body, involving the muscles which are used throughout the speech. Giving up this product, or at least reducing your use of it, might be advantageous.

Some individuals have a comparable response to sugar. While this is not true for everybody, it deserves examining if you have a stuttering issue. Decreasing the amount of sugar in your diet might help you to end up being calmer. You can try it and see if it works for you!

Chapter 7: Is Avoidance a Useful Strategy?

When it pertains to the topic of stuttering, some techniques are really useful to some individuals, while not as helpful for others. This is since each person is an individual, and everyone's stuttering issue is distinct to him or her. The only way to understand for sure which methods are going to work for you is to give them all a shot and see what works for you.

Avoidance is a controversial issue. Some individuals insist it works rather well, while others do not find it as handy. The controversy is in whether avoidance is a suitable method for managing a stuttering issue. If you are serious about discovering techniques that work, it is an excellent idea to overlook that whole controversy and try it for yourself and see what you make of it.

The standard way avoidance is practiced is to place words that are simple to speak in place of those which are not so simple to speak. If you have actually been bothered by your stuttering to the extent of checking out this book, you are most likely already aware of the distinction. You have seen that numerous words seem to stream rather effortlessly, while others end up being "stuck" or repeat. You might have additionally observed that particular sounds, or particular letters of the alphabet, are more annoying than others.

When you are considering this method, you might want to take a look at both sides of the problem. This can help you to choose whether it is right for you, and what you might be handling when you try it. Initially, practicing avoidance can help you to feel more in control of your speech in general. When you understand what you want to say, and how you intend to say it, it can offer you a decided benefit. Instead of questioning and stressing, you will remain in control.

Nevertheless, avoidance can additionally have unfavorable ramifications. When you approach talking to somebody in this way, you might end up being more uncomfortable. For some individuals, this can backfire; for others, it is not an issue at all.

If you want to give this method a shot, put a little time into the "demons" of your speech. When you understand which words, sounds, and letters are usually at fault for creating a stutter, you can select a different word that means the same thing. You are going to discover that language is a wonderful thing without a doubt-- there is a synonym, or a related word, for each word you wish to say! For instance, if the word "box" is among your speech demons, try saying "container" as an alternative. You can expand your vocabulary, while learning a new method by which to manage your stutter.

Chapter 8: Establish the Habit of Speaking Slowly

You might already understand that when your words come out in an out of breath rush, it makes your stutter even worse. You begin to say a word, and numerous other words appear to tumble after, like a domino-effect. Establishing the habit of speaking slowly is a method that can assist you in managing your stutter.

Knowing how to speak slowly is not really hard. If you have actually not yet cultivated this habit, now is a great time to start. When you wish to speak, take a minute to prepare yourself. Form each word gradually, and make it possible for each word to stream smoothly and naturally. Instead of remaining in a rush to get a total sentence out, consider each word as streaming from you to your listener.

When you discover that the other individual is listening to whatever you are saying, this can aid you to speak gradually. Interaction is meant to be a favorable experience. It is far more than just exchanging words, or waiting for your opportunity to speak. It is among the very best ways to delight in and value the company of another individual-- by exchanging ideas, feelings, thoughts, and information. Keeping these concepts at the base of your verbal interaction can be considerably helpful in keeping it in perspective.

This point of view can additionally help you in discovering how to speak slowly. You do not need to get your words out rapidly since the other individual is listening and appreciates everything you say! He or she is genuinely interested! When you think of it in this manner, it ought to provide you with a reason to stop for a minute and think. You might be valuing your verbal interactions much more. Equally crucial, if you consider this when you are preparing to have a conversation with somebody, it can help you to manage your stutter. As your words stream smoothly and gradually, you are going to see how it benefits your speech.

Chapter 9: How Relaxation Can Aid You to Manage Your Stutter

Relaxation has a dual function in managing stuttering. It works on both the body and the mind simultaneously. You might not have actually considered this before, and you might not know of the numerous favorable impacts relaxation can have on you and your wellbeing.

Initially, relaxation impacts every part of your body-- your whole system. This consists of all of the muscles that are utilized when you speak. From the muscles in your throat to that fantastic diaphragm, the more relaxed your body is, the easier the words are going to stream. Relaxed muscles imply smoother speech; and smoother speech implies less chance of stuttering.

Second, relaxation impacts the mind. Even if you currently understand this, you might not have thought of how it is linked to your speech. The mind that is relaxed is better focused and more controlled. It is less troubled by little inconveniences, which produce uneasiness, stress, and self-consciousness. In turn, when the mind is relaxed and at ease, you are less likely to experience serious stuttering.

How do you discover how to unwind, so that you can enjoy these benefits? It is not difficult, even if you have a hectic pace or lifestyle in which it seems that everything will collapse if you stop. You can start with slow, deep breathing. Imagine yourself in a wonderful, calm environment, where everything is tranquil and serene. Permit yourself the luxury of dwelling in these types of thoughts occasionally, throughout your day.

After you have actually discovered how to do this, you can take your brand-new practice with you when you have to interact with other individuals. Before you start to speak, picture your calm atmosphere. Allow the soothing relaxation to fill your mind and to fill your body. Not just will you feel more comfortable, even in business or social circumstances, you actually are going to be more at ease. Your body and mind will appreciate the impacts of relaxation and will aid you in managing your stutter.

Chapter 10: Establish Self-confidence in Your Speech

The more confident you are, the less difficulty you are going to have with stuttering. This consists of confidence in yourself, along with self-confidence in your speech. If you have actually been troubled by stuttering for a long time, it might require time and effort to establish this self-confidence. The rewards are going to be worth the effort you invest in it.

The more deserving and important you understand you are as an individual, the easier it will be to establish self-confidence in yourself. You can start by telling yourself that whatever you intend to state is important and that your listeners wish to hear from you. Even if you are naturally shy, this can aid you to end up being more assertive. When you go into the habit of showing a positive mindset, it will begin to increase the self-confidence you have in yourself. You will quickly see other individuals reacting in a favorable manner to the brand-new you!

Establishing self-confidence in your speech can be just as effortless. It demands some practice, naturally, however discovering how to do it is rather straightforward. You can even start to apply self-confidence to your speech before you truly have it. This implies that even if you are not yet sure of yourself. When you speak as if you are sure about your capabilities, it is going to come true.

Self-confidence in speech suggests beginning whatever you want to say as plainly and concisely as possible. Tell yourself that you are well-informed about the subject you are discussing and that it is necessary for you to say it. This sensation of authority is going to make you confident about what you are saying. Let your words stream effortlessly, with the exact same air of authority and self-confidence. Allow your words to advance naturally, one by one. While practicing the breathing method, you have actually already found out how to speak without stopping to pause on individual words.

When you have actually established this sort of self-confidence, you are going to be less likely to trip up on those frustrating words. With practice, your stutter might end up being a distant memory.

Chapter 11: Does Analyzing Help-- or Does it Make Stuttering Worse?

You might have heard of analyzing. You might have tried it yourself. The truth is that in numerous cases, it can aggravate stuttering. While this book is supplying you with practical methods that can aid you in managing your stutter, it ought to be kept in mind that this common technique is seldom in a stutterer's best interest.

Analyzing is typically done by putting effort and time into attempting to determine the issue, in the hope of alleviating it. Analyzing can consist of studying the vocabulary one regularly uses, looking for those pesky "demon" words. It can additionally consist of taking special note of the parts of one's body and muscles one utilizes throughout the daily speech.

The unfavorable element of analyzing in this way is it highlights the issue, instead of constructive solutions. You might find yourself so mindful of problematic words that it increases your stuttering. You might end up being so concentrated on your muscles that it, in fact, impedes your capability to speak plainly. You can end up being so uneasy that your stuttering gets worse.

You are currently knowledgeable about the issue. After all, you have actually been dealing with it for a very long time. Your objective ought to be to gain control of your stutter so that you can be pleased with your capability to communicate successfully. Putting an excessive focus on your stutter is not the best way to continue. Rather, recognizing that your issue can be conquered and that you can do it, will yield more successful outcomes. Instead of living in the issue, you will be living in the solution-- making the very most of all of your verbal interactions.

Chapter 12: Taking a Tip from a Celebrity

Depending upon your age and interest in country music, you might be familiar with Mel Tillis. He has actually been among the most popular country music singers throughout the last couple of decades. A truth that many individuals do not know is that Mel Tillis has had difficulty with stuttering throughout his lifetime!

Mel Tillis has given interviews in the past, mentioning that while his speech consists of stuttering, it is not present the moment he sings. Not only has this helped him to establish self-confidence, it helped him to turn into one of the best-loved singers in country music.

You may like to give this a shot, too. You can begin with one of your favorite singers, somebody of your gender whose voice resembles your own. Purchase one of the person's CD's, and accompany him or her throughout songs you enjoy. After you have ended up being familiar with your singing voice, you might feel ready to sing along.

You might discover that your singing voice is as clear and stunning, and as stutter-free, as Mel Tillis's singing voice. This can be a terrific way to increase your self-confidence. The abler you are to sing without that obvious stutter, the more confident you are going to be in your routine verbal communications.

This is an enjoyable way to gain control of your stutter. While the other methods call for practice, work, and effort, you are going to certainly find this technique to be more satisfying. You might even establish a new pastime. You may not become a star like Mel Tillis, however, you can take a suggestion from him to find out how to manage your stutter.

Chapter 13: Can Medication Help?

You might be at wit's end over your stuttering. Maybe you have attempted these or other techniques and discovered that absolutely nothing works as effectively as you had hoped. Maybe aggravation, fear, or concern is getting in the way of managing your stutter. You might be questioning if the medication can fix the issue, or at the very least, alleviate it.

An excellent guideline is to rule out medication unless your stuttering is so serious that natural methods do not help. While some individuals may disagree, utilizing any kind of medication for stuttering ought to just be considered as a last option. Unless your stuttering is being brought on by a medical issue that requires your physician's assessment and suggestions, depending on natural techniques is much better than depending on pharmaceuticals.

If you are thinking about medication, it is important for you to seek your doctor's guidance. Under no circumstances should you ever try to self-medicate. Utilizing any sort of pharmaceutical product without your physician's approval can be extremely harmful. In addition, devices and home remedies ought to additionally be avoided. You desire relief from your stutter, however taking chances with your health is never ever the best option.

This chapter will offer you a summary of the medications which are typically utilized to alleviate or manage stuttering. Numerous physicians agree that their usage for this purpose is extremely questionable. If you are considering attempting medication to manage your stutter, just your own physician can suggest a medication for you.

Zyprexa has a moderate success rate in dealing with stuttering. This drug is mainly utilized for dealing with schizophrenia and other comparable conditions. The experiences of individuals who have actually utilized Zyprexa for stuttering range from a high degree of satisfaction with the outcomes to little impact at all. Zyprexa is a dopamine-blocker drug. Its side effects can vary from decreasing awareness to weight gain.

There are a variety of medical conditions that contraindicate the use of Zyprexa, so it must never ever be utilized without your doctor having a complete understanding of your medical history. A lesser-known reality about Zyprexa is that its tablet form consists of aspartame, making it hazardous for people who have phenylketonuria (typically called PKU).

While some doctors disagree with the practice of prescribing tranquilizers as a remedy for stuttering, others think that they can be helpful. The overall consensus among those who consider it a proper form of treatment is that decreasing the individual's anxiety and uneasiness will, in turn, decrease his stuttering.

Although the possible side effects of tranquilizers can vary from slight to extreme, an additional element is their potential to cause addiction. Addiction to tranquilizers is frequent, and withdrawal from these drugs is frequently tough and agonizing. If your physician feels that this is the appropriate type of treatment for you, your use of tranquilizers needs to be thoroughly and regularly tracked.

Some doctors think that antidepressants can aid in alleviating stuttering. Studies had actually revealed that while some individuals do get relief from this type of treatment, others experience worse stuttering than they had before the treatment started. As is the problem with any pharmaceutical preparation, making use of antidepressants needs to be decided on a case-by-case basis. Even with your medical history in hand, your physician might not have the ability to identify beforehand whether these drugs are going to assist you or whether your stuttering will worsen.

There are a number of various antidepressants presently available. While the negative side effects of antidepressants can vary from sleep disruptions to sexual problems and others, the side effects an individual experiences from using antidepressants is mainly based upon his own individual system. They can vary from extremely slight to extreme. Some individuals discover the side effects of antidepressants to be just reasonably irritating, while others consider the negative side effects more unbearable than the initial issue.

Two drugs presently on the marketplace, which show a significant amount of promise in dealing with stuttering are Haldol and Risperdal. Both of these drugs are dopamine-blockers. While they both have the capacity of causing significant side-effects in some patients, studies have actually revealed these medications to have up to a fifty-percent success rate when utilized to deal with stuttering.

Numerous doctors agree that dopamine-blocking drugs are the method of choice when utilizing medication to deal with stuttering. Nevertheless, as this has actually not been in practice for very long, it is smart to think about the ramifications of this truth before becoming quick to have a go at medication. While choosing whether the possibility of attaining a measure of relief from stuttering is worth running the risk of the variety of prospective side-effects while using a medication might be hard enough, the absence of existing information on prospective long-lasting side-effects can make this decision even tougher.

You want to remedy for your stutter. You might want to go to any lengths to be without the issue. For the sake of both your short-term and long-term health, you must not be too swift to choose that medication is the response. As any pharmaceutical preparation has the potential to result in problems, you need to plainly evaluate both the advantages and the dangers. You need to look for the guidance of a qualified doctor additionally.

The most reasonable approach to utilizing the medication for the treatment of stuttering is to consider it just as the last option. Unless all of the natural techniques for managing your stutter have actually fallen short, and you have actually discovered that your stuttering disrupts your life to the extent that you can not deal with it, medication ought to be avoided.

This chapter has been featured in this book since many individuals are quick to consider medication as an excellent, quick, miracle-cure. They do not recognize how hazardous medication can be to their health. Regrettably, some capable doctors additionally have the viewpoint that medication is the best strategy, without first examining all of the options.

When you have all of these truths, you are going to be in the very best position to decide what is right for you. You do not need to put unneeded risks on your health in order to alleviate your stutter. Almost everybody can attain outcomes which they are pleased with, without turning to medication.

Chapter 14: Special Needs: Stuttering in Kids

You might have bought this book in the hope of aiding your kid with a stuttering issue. While much of the methods explained in this book are equally suitable for kids, the kid who stutters has special needs which additionally need to be attended to.

A youngster who stutters remains in a particularly vulnerable position. Whether he is a young kid or a teen, stuttering can have more impact on a kid than on an adult. When you take your kid's special needs into consideration, the methods in this book are going to be more valuable to him.

The most substantial impact stuttering has on a kid is in his relations with other individuals, particularly his peers. Kids of all ages are typically subjected to mock when they show any sort of issue which separates them from their peers. A speech impediment like stuttering can hinder a kid's capability to communicate with his peers. He might be targeted for ridicule and bullying.

This special issue can make it far tougher for the kid to make buddies. It can stand in the way of healthy socializing. It is not unusual for a kid who stutters to end up being isolated and depressed. He might be afraid of simple interaction, and incredibly uneasy. His self-confidence can be much lower than that of a non-stuttering kid; he might establish an unfavorable opinion of himself. He might additionally worry about carrying his stuttering with him for the remainder of his life.

These problems are why stuttering needs to be dealt with as quickly as you recognize it in your kid. The quicker you start to aid him in managing his stutter, the better his overall quality of life will be. Oftentimes, stuttering is rather visible long before a kid starts school. In other circumstances, it is not obvious until he is older.

Building your kid's self-confidence works together with aiding him to manage his stutter. While it ought to be apparent, parents and other grownups must never ever make the mistake of shaming a kid about his stuttering. The more of a problem you make about his stuttering, the worse he is going to feel about himself. This, in turn, can lead to his stuttering worsening. He might feel that he is to blame for his issue, which is going to make it more intense.

While grownups might not be hurt by making a joke of stuttering, this is seldom the case for kids. Even the most well-meaning siblings can hamper a kid's progress in managing a stutter by making "jokes" about it. It is no laughing matter to the child who stutters. Sarcasm and jokes can be ravaging to the kid.

The kid who stutters needs to understand that you and the other individuals in his life are encouraging. He has to understand that he is not rejected, nor looked down on, over his issue. He needs to understand that he is accepted and liked, just as he is-- stuttering included. This type of unconditional love and approval will offer a strong base for assisting him in managing his stutter without the kid seeing the issue as a reflection of himself.

Offering a calm environment is the very best way to start helping your kid to manage his stutter. In cases of extremely young kids, much of the techniques explained in this book could be presented as games. Instead of presenting a method as something which he needs to perform in order to conquer an issue, letting him see a method as enjoyable and pleasurable will produce the very best outcomes

Teaching a kid methods to aid him in managing his stutter can be more unpleasant and discouraging for the adult than it is for the child. He might not be cooperative, or you might not see any clear outcomes. It is vital that you do not become demanding, or push him to practice a method. It is additionally important for you to not communicate your disappointment when you believe a method is worthless. Both of these mistakes can rapidly backfire. They can cause him to quit.

Convincing your kid that discovering methods to manage his stutter is something which he, in fact, wishes to do is not as tough as it might sound. The majority of parents already have practice in encouraging their kids that particular things are a good idea. When methods for managing stuttering are presented in a light-hearted, enjoyable manner, your child will generally comply just since he wishes to comply.

While a parent might believe that rewarding a kid for learning a method is a favorable approach, it frequently is not. If your kid ends up being acclimated to rewards, this can make it even harder for him when he is not effective. He might even feel that he is being penalized for slipping up-- and for not being excellent. When finding out how to manage a stutter, mistakes are as common in kids as they are in grownups. Merely letting him understand that you are pleased with his efforts, despite the outcomes, is far better than providing him with rewards. A kid will be eager to discover a brand-new ability when he sees that his efforts are valued.

When parents see their kid stuttering, they frequently freak out. This can indicate rushing him to his pediatrician, making appointments to see speech therapists, and even thinking about medication. You can spare both yourself and your kid from a great deal of unneeded irritation by not being too fast to conclude that he will be a lifelong stutterer without instant intervention.

The truth is that numerous kids stutter sometimes. Some really young kids stutter when they are at first finding out verbal abilities; others stutter when they are very nervous, exhausted, or feel overloaded. In the interest of your kid's psychological health, you ought to resist seeing these types of circumstances as potentially-serious issues. If you are your kid's primary caretaker, it should not be tough to figure out whether he is showing a speech impediment or whether it is simply a phase.

Talking about the issue of stuttering in kids additionally consists of the element of medication. As parents are frequently not well-informed about this, it needs to be kept in mind that some medications which are frequently provided to kids can cause them to stutter, even when they do not have a real speech impediment.

Ritalin, which is typically prescribed for such conditions as ADHD and ADD, is among the greatest offenders. If you observe stuttering in a kid who is taking this or other medications, it must be brought to the attention of his physician. The medication might be the reason for his stuttering. If so, calibrating the dose or switching medications can get rid of his stuttering completely. Nevertheless, this must not be tried without your physician's recommendation.

The kid who stutters is just as ordinary as other kids. The way he is treated in his daily life should highlight this truth. Although stuttering can be hazardous to a kid's self-confidence and social development, it is not nearly as hazardous as making an issue of the problem. The kid who understands that he is loved and accepted precisely as he is, while being supplied with methods to aid him to manage his stutter in the most satisfying manner possible, is the kid who is more than likely to be prosperous.

Chapter 15: Is a Speech Therapist Necessary?

Whether you are trying to find help for yourself or for your kid, you might be considering requesting help from a speech therapist. You might question if this is the right choice. There are a number of points to think about when choosing if you or your kid should go to a speech therapist.

One example in which speaking with a speech therapist is a legitimate method is if stuttering is so serious that it affects your functioning. If it is so severe that it is disruptive to your daily life, help from a specialist might be in order. Whether the stuttering has actually been a long-lasting issue, or whether its start has been unexpected, a speech therapist can be valuable.

A 2nd scenario is if all methods and approaches for managing your stutter have stopped working. Although the methods explained in this book are simple to learn and effective for many individuals, they might not be as helpful for you. If you have actually put your best effort into these methods, and have discovered no remedy for your stuttering, a visit to a speech therapist might be in your best interest.

Another scenario that makes seeking advice from a speech therapist a smart choice is if your stuttering is connected to any medical or mental cause. In these circumstances, managing your stutter by yourself might be unattainable. If a preexisting medical or mental condition is discovered to be at the root of your stutter, a speech therapist can direct you to the professional help that is suitable for you.

While seeking advice from a speech therapist is not needed for the majority of instances of youth or teen stuttering, there are scenarios in which it is the very best strategy. The kid whose stutter is so serious that no methods offer any relief is among these circumstances.

The kid whose stutter puts an excessive burden on his daily life is another. For the most part, kids react to natural techniques along with grownups. Nevertheless, if they do not work for your kid, taking him to a speech therapist could be in his best interest.

The kid who declines to comply in finding out how to manage his stutter is another situation that needs a speech therapist. This does not suggest hurrying to make an appointment as soon as your kid refuses to comply. You should expect some degree of boredom or disinterest when teaching him these new ideas. The kid who flatly refuses to cooperate at all, shows anger or animosity at your efforts to help, or strongly believes that absolutely nothing will work, can benefit from seeing a speech therapist. The child who shows mental issues related to his stutter can additionally benefit from seeing a specialist. In these instances, his pediatrician or your family doctor can suggest a therapist who can aid him.

If you or your kid is going to be seeing a speech therapist, these visits must not be any more disruptive to daily life than needed. The kid who sees a therapist might resent putting his time into it, and might feel that this course of action is an unfavorable reflection on himself. The very best technique for handling these issues effectively is to present the visits in a favorable light. If he sees his speech therapist as a pal, and as a nice person who really wishes to assist him, he can eagerly anticipate the visits and benefit from them a lot more.

Speech therapists can be expensive. If this is a problem for you, you need to have all of the facts before you make a dedication. You can check to see if your insurance is going to cover a speech therapist or ask if he or she is going to accept a sensible payment plan. The cost must not be the deciding factor in whether to look for assistance from a professional.

Your pediatrician or family physician is the very best resource for finding a speech therapist. He understands your specific circumstance and can suggest the therapist who is right for you. Do not be reluctant in requesting his guidance.

For the most part, stuttering can be managed solely by discovering these simple methods and applying them to your daily speech. Nevertheless, if you or your kid are in one of these special scenarios, a professional speech therapist can be significantly helpful. The sooner you request assistance, the quicker you can get the stutter under control.

Chapter 16: Progress, Not Perfection

Whenever you are learning something brand-new, success does not come immediately. Expecting overnight outcomes, or expecting perfection, is a recipe for catastrophe. This is among the most crucial points to keep in mind when you are finding out how to manage your stutter.

Expecting too much, prematurely, or expecting that you are never going to stutter again, puts excessive pressure on yourself. With this approach, you might end up being incredibly dissuaded and irritated when you do not attain the outcomes you desire as swiftly as you had hoped. This sort of frustration can lead you to stop before you get favorable outcomes. It can additionally cause you to see a mistake or a small obstacle as a complete failure. You want to stay away from this sort of pressure if you genuinely want to be successful!

When you think about finding out how to manage your stutter in regards to learning a brand-new skill, both the outcomes and your mindset will be much better. As getting to know anything brand-new requires time, practice, and even trial-and-error, this is additionally the case with finding out how to manage your stutter. Some methods will work better for you than others; some methods will not be useful for you; and others are going to provide you with outstanding outcomes. If you want to make that dedication, you can attain success.

Patience is the needed key in finding out how to manage your stutter. You need to be willing to put your time into learning a technique, and applying it to your daily exchanges. When you slip up, you need to have the ability to let it go without letting it bother you. This is how to make progress.

Progress is not a promise of perfection. Even after you have actually mastered a method and put it into practice, you might still experience a mistake. You might have felt that you were entirely devoid of your stutter, just to have it happen at the most bothersome time. Instead of ending up being flustered, or worrying that you have actually not achieved anything, lightheartedly brushing it off is a far better strategy. You might not be perfect, yet you are still successful!

The idea of "progress- not perfection" is a lot more legitimate for the kid who stutters. As kids are more naturally inclined to see a small obstacle or mistake as a total disaster, teaching him to see his achievements for how remarkable they are is the most useful approach.

You can start by instilling this principle before you begin to teach him the methods to manage his stutter. Nothing genuinely worthwhile was ever achieved overnight, and even in the very best situations, mistakes do happen. When he is equipped with these ideas before he begins discovering the methods, he is ready for success and will value it every step of the way.

Stuttering does not need to play a big part in your life. It does not need to hinder your communications with other individuals, nor impact the way you think of yourself. All it takes is time, effort, and dedication to learn these simple methods. When you see which methods work ideally for you, practicing them will offer you a brand-new, positive view of your capability to speak plainly in social scenarios. Applying them regularly whenever you communicate verbally with other individuals will provide you with more self-confidence than you have ever had before.

Knowing how to manage your stutter is your very first step to a better, more satisfying life. The more you practice, the more progress you are going to make-- and this is the best description of real success!

I hope that you enjoyed reading through this book and that you have found it useful. If you want to share your thoughts on this book, you can do so by leaving a review on the Amazon page. Have a great rest of the day.